THE PATH OF THE SOUL

Some further books of White Eagle's teaching.

THE PATH OF THE SOUL

WHITE EAGLE

THE GREAT INITIATIONS
OF EVERY MAN

THE WHITE EAGLE PUBLISHING TRUST

LISS · HAMPSHIRE · ENGLAND

MCMLXXIX

First Edition: September 1959
Reprinted: May 1972
Reprinted: August 1975
Reprinted: March 1979

© *Copyright, The White Eagle Publishing Trust, 1959*

ISBN 0 85487 020 2

Printed in Great Britain by
FLETCHER AND SON LTD, NORWICH

CONTENTS

∽

Introduction

'Path' and 'Soul' are words which need defining. The word 'Soul' throughout this book stands for our human self—the inner self to which we wake each day, that self which is a compendium of all our likes and dislikes, our hopes and fears, our kindnesses, unselfishness, forbearance —or of our meannesses, egotism, irritability; in other words, our character. But the term largely excludes our bodily self. None of this body's burden and complaint is meant by or included in the word 'Soul,' which is that tender *inside self*, our inner feelings and thoughts which we hide or seclude from the intrusion of most people—our natural, our real, our *inner* self. It is this part of us which will survive death.

For this soul there is a very definite 'Path' which it should begin to follow in life here and now. It will be exceedingly unwise to arrive on the further shore of the next world minus, so to speak, a passport, and without any preparation. Each human soul is given the opportunity of following this path of spiritual progression and unfoldment and making ready for its journey to happier climes. This journey is called 'The Path' throughout this book. It does not begin with incarnation nor end with physical death; it continues onward into the unknown.

Every path should be signposted accurately and clearly if people are to arrive anywhere. This particular Path, of all paths the most important because it awaits every wayfarer, is no exception. Jesus Christ is here our signpost, the way-shower. His is that way of truth and life. But not always according to the letter, as recorded in the Gospels. The letter may have value, truth of a sort; but far exceeding in value and truth is the underlying meaning of these Gospels; so that Jesus' life among men, with all its major issues such as birth, baptism, temptation, transfiguration, crucifixion and resurrection, reveals itself as a great parable most clearly setting forth the Path which all souls of men will ultimately have to tread.

The contents of this book have come from one who is a member of a great brotherhood, the White Brotherhood beyond death which is striving to bring salvation to mankind.

The communicator is known as White Eagle. He is the guide and teacher of Mrs. Grace Cooke, through whom these words were spoken. Authority and power can only be established on truth. The book seeks no other criterion. If the words make clear much that hitherto has been deeply puzzling and mysterious in the four Gospels, then its truth has established itself and the reader will find the Path open and a guide awaiting him.

I

The Preparation

Some of our readers may wonder why we shall so
often refer to the four Gospels during this series
of messages. We do so because they contain many
essential truths concerning man's spiritual unfoldment, from its beginning to its end; so that
the more one ponders over these writings, the
deeper one goes into the Ancient Wisdom and
into a knowledge which every living soul is consciously or unconsciously seeking. For this knowledge can unveil the nature of life in the heaven
worlds and also give new understanding of the
value of every detail and happening which goes to
make up everyday life on earth. Man needs not
only the 'vision glorious' but also sufficient wisdom to bring this knowledge through into his
mundane life; which should become more wisely
directed and influenced by the vision he has seen,
so that the light of his knowledge radiates not
through his character alone, but also refines the
substance of his physical body.

In addition, if we can attune ourselves so that
we habitually express or manifest something of
divine truth in daily life, we shall be preparing

ourselves for the supreme initiation. Some people think that initiation involves going through a ceremony of some kind, and this in a sense is true. The initiation we have in mind, however, is something which is taking place over a long period, during which the soul quickens and earnestly endeavours to practise the spiritual truths which it has acquired. In this case the soul will prepare itself for and pass initiation after initiation. On the other hand, as is too often the case, the man will remain unaware, wrapped up in his earthly self and be 'spiritually dead'—in fact, as the Bible says, be one of 'the dead who know not anything.' The spiritually dead cannot comprehend or even glimpse truth; they live in a state of darkness.

There are two kinds of people—those who know and those who do not know; those who have perceived reality, and those who are still blind to the real life. Some people cling to the idea that initiation can come about only by recognised stages—say, by attaining to what is called the first, second, third, or fourth, or even the thirty-third degree. This is not always so; by searching your own inner experience, you may find that you have been preparing for a number of degrees at the same time, but are not yet complete in any one of them. In other words, you are training first on one level for a period and then on another;

so we find that the soul, through contact with its brother man, and through all the experiences of its incarnation, is preparing for the supreme initiation throughout human life. This we know as the Christ initiation, or initiation into the full power and consciousness of the divine, the Christ light, which is called the Son of God.

The life of Jesus the Christ as pictured in the Gospels is also the story of the life of every soul. It presents the story of the major spiritual experiences which will await every aspirant seeking knowledge and wisdom, who will himself in turn pass through temptation and whose soul will even endure crucifixion and attain resurrection —for these experiences can take many different forms. This you should bear in mind whenever you study and meditate upon the four Gospels, more particularly that of St. John. Remember too that religions throughout all time have presented this esoteric knowledge concerning man's birth or descent into matter, his experiences through living imprisoned in the flesh, and his arising from matter—or his rising from the 'floor' into the 'chair,' as it is sometimes called—into the place of command or mastership.

All religions teach these truths according to the understanding of their adherents. Today much of this teaching may appear crude or at least elementary; this is because the inner truth has vanished and only the shell has been retained. Only the earnest seeker can still descend into the vault where truth lies buried and there uncover spiritual treasure. But to obtain this treasure demands far more than mere exercise of intellect. Not by intellectual prowess alone can these mysteries be uncovered, but through daily practice of the presence of God. This may sound obvious; you may have heard it often before. But when the soul absorbs divine light through constant meditation upon the Light, and through opening the heart in compassion, tenderness and love towards all life, then the veil is drawn aside, and the soul *becomes* truth, *becomes* light; and this light within the soul will never again depart from it.

Some of your own personal experiences have already proved this to be true. For when carried away by joy or overwrought by pain, or at any time when you are emotionally overstressed, you are like a frail boat tossed about in a storm. Yet within everyone waits the sleeping Master, the indwelling Christ. When at last you call upon Him in your distress, crying, 'Master, help me!' you do not appeal to any outside power or person, but to the Christ within. With all your heart you cry, 'O Thou who art light and power and love, come to my aid!' Then tranquillity steals over you. You are aware of an indwelling strength and become still. Perhaps later, when you have trained yourself by meditation, you will have power to rise as on a shaft of light to function on a plane superior to this, and looking down upon your emotional disturbance, see what it really is.

This control over emotion, anger and fear is one of the earliest degrees of initiation—and this not by repression but by sublimation of these emotions which can be seen by the clairvoyant darting through the aura as tongues of flame. All the unruly emotions can be subdued and transmuted by the Christ within, and any passion that has been aroused, instead of injuring and destroying—for it *can* destroy—goes forth transmuted into love, with power to heal, to bless, to lighten the burdens of the world, manifesting amid the darkness as a pure white light.

Nothing causes a more severe reaction upon the physical body than violent emotion. You may not always recognise this as a real cause of subsequent illness; you suffer bodily pain, and you attribute it to a physical origin. The aspirant, however, must be prepared to acknowledge that emotions which can shatter man's finer bodies must eventually cause ill health in either minor or major degrees. Therefore control of a man's emotional body, and the transmutation of his lower passions into the higher, are certain to produce an effect upon health; and the soul which lives close to the Christ light usually acquires a harmonious and healthy body.

Here we must add that nobody, no matter whether discarnate or incarnate, can judge another. Indeed, no initiate will dare to judge, but simply gives forth love and healing from his own aura to the person concerned, without criticism or question, well understanding that a human being can only go forward step by step, learning by trial and error, gradually acquiring wisdom, self-control, and spiritual illumination. Even so, often when the soul appears to be almost perfect some inharmony may remain, and this may manifest in some bodily disease, however slight, until that inharmony has been transmuted.

The soul must acquire complete dispassion, meeting every event of human life with tranquillity, knowing that everything which happens results either from some preceding failure or some achievement of its own, and that all works together for good. We may dislike some particular happening. We may exclaim, 'This sorrow will break me! How can a God of love send me these manifold afflictions?' But God's love is so much greater than any of our poor human conceptions of love, and God sends these happenings into a human life in order to afford the soul an opportunity to strengthen itself, so that it may learn to meet all the experiences of life with tranquillity, never doubting that whatever happens is for its eventual good.

The Bible records many stories of men who were tested, seemingly almost beyond endurance. Such was Job, who underwent many bitter sorrows and much suffering until everything he possessed was at last taken from him. Yet throughout his trial he still trusted his Father God, and so he passed his test. He was assured that whatever happened was either because he had deserved it, or was something which had come to test him before his final initiation.

From this instance and others which could be cited you may gather that the great and advanced soul keeps true to its awareness that God is altogether good, that God visits apparent sufferings upon His children only out of love. Indeed, only through undergoing such experiences with fortitude does the soul learn in practice to stand fast. My brethren, pray that through life's experiences you may find this inner poise and the real inner strength which inspires the greatest courage. Know that nothing has power to destroy the eternal love, the living flame within; that nothing matters so long as you know God or Christ within you.

The Bible bids us lay up our treasure in heaven, in the assurance that when the soul grows rich within it becomes possessed of priceless wealth that nothing can destroy or take away.

Now, step by step, we shall amplify these teachings concerning the soul's awakening, the soul's initiation. We shall see how closely these are related not only to the Christian doctrine but also to other religions throughout the ages—realising that this is indeed the Ancient Wisdom, the jewel of truth possessing many facets. But we would emphasise that this knowledge is of very little use if the aspirant only becomes engrossed intellectually; there must come a realisation of the light which burns within and a *becoming* of that light; or readjustment of the life so that it becomes *lived in light*.

2

The Water Initiation

(I)

We come from the spiritual realms to try to impart some of the knowledge which we ourselves have found. We cannot travel your path, or live your life for you, but we can act as a signpost, by telling you from the result of our own experience whither that path will lead you. The freewill choice as to the direction you will follow will still be yours, for you have to learn to develop and use the qualities of discernment and discrimination. One thing, however, is quite certain: truth of this nature can only be discerned from the innermost, from the pure spirit within man. This is why the Master so clearly advised his followers to become 'as little children,' which means to draw aside from the promptings of the earthly or reasoning mind. You will say, 'But surely our reason is given us to use?' Yes, your reason has its own special purpose, but it cannot enable you to discern spiritual truth. Spiritual truth, when revealed to the vision of the spirit by the Christ within, will pass the most searching test of reason, for being complete and unanswerable it satisfies all the yearnings of man's being.

We are now going to deal specifically with the Water Initiation, called by some 'baptism by water.' By this we do not mean the baptism of infants as is customary in a church, but what we may call 'soul baptism.'

For it is not only the cleansing water, but the human soul itself which is signified by the water element. In the Bible and also in other mystical revelations 'the waters' signify the psyche, the soul of man. The waters of the soul, which can be either calm and still and so reflect the heavens, or else so rough and turbulent that they reflect nothing, must be brought under the control of the Master. Before a soul can proceed on the path of initiation, the Christ within must discipline that soul and make it calm enough to reflect the true image of the higher worlds. This was the first initiation undergone by Jesus. You ask, 'But why did such a being as Jesus need any kind of initiation—surely He was beyond our limitations?' But Jesus the Christ was also Jesus the Man, and therefore had to undergo exactly the same training and follow the same path that all must follow. But remember also that although true in itself this story is also an *allegory* depicting the life of every soul. Every soul must eventually be 'baptised' or cleansed emotionally. Again, we do not refer to the ceremony of baptism in any church—

we are speaking of certain inner experiences which await every soul.

If you read the account of John the Baptist in the Gospels, you will notice that the place in which he dwelt is described as a wilderness—the wilderness of the world, the chaotic condition of man's collective soul. We are all in a wilderness within until we begin to discipline ourselves and turn our soul-wilderness into a beautiful garden. The term 'wilderness' in fact stands for the state of chaos, loneliness and unhappiness which is the lot of the soul before it is awakened.

The meaning of the name John is 'the gift of God.' God sends to the soul of man the gift of a teacher. When the soul is ready to be baptised, the teacher is there, to show the soul what it longs to know; thus John, the gift of God, was ready to teach those who came to be cleansed and purified. (Matthew iii, 5, 6.)

Note also the description of John's raiment and the way he lived, for this too has an inner meaning. Any man ready to learn must be clothed with humility, and be prepared to eat very simple food. Some are not satisfied unless they can devour an intellectual feast, at which they eat grossly and suffer afterwards. Having swallowed, in a mental and spiritual sense, more than they can stomach, they later turn away in discomfort from their spiritual aspiration. But the true aspirant is clothed with humility, and prepared to nurture his spirit upon simple foods.

John is said to have called his people to repent, but what *is* repentance? Does it mean no more than saying, 'O, I am sorry,' promising that such a thing will not happen again, and afterwards doing exactly this again—as we all do, many, many times? No: repentance means real effort and real determination to change oneself and not again to miss the mark. We would say that sin is a failure to go direct to the truth. When striking out his first furrow across a field a ploughman has always to keep his eye fixed upon a distant marking-post. If his eye wanders he cannot drive a straight furrow. This applies also to our own actions, particularly to our relations with our brother men. We sin when we fail to drive a straight furrow to the marking-post. Some people may protest that they have always lived a good life, and how can they then have sinned? The answer is that every time the soul does not live truth from its innermost being, it is sinning. Some bodily sins we would not call sins at all. Sin is the failure of the soul to live truly, to express truth in thought and word and deed.

To be always true is most difficult. Nevertheless, whenever a soul fails to be true, it is guilty of sin; so we begin to see how many of us are sinners, simply through weakness or sloth.

*And Jesus, when he was baptised, went up straightway
out of the water: and, lo, the heavens were opened unto him,
and he saw the Spirit of God descending like a dove, and light-
ing upon him: and lo, a voice from heaven, saying, This is my
beloved Son, in whom I am well pleased.* (Matthew iii,
16-17.)

Now, when the soul has been mystically baptised, it has passed the Water Initiation, which
means that it has become disciplined and no
longer gives way to anger, fear, or passion.
Having undergone its test, it has learned how
to remain tranquil. It has overcome all hasty
judgments, all angry passion, all subtle fear and
anxiety. In this state the soul is at last able to see
the vision and hear the voice of God. How could
it hope to hear before, when it was making too
much noise within itself? But when at last it
becomes like a calm lake shining beneath the sun
or moon, then the heavens reflect their glory in
the waters of the soul. Thus the soul when in
meditation reflects the heavens—a true, not a
false reflection, which is frequently the case when
there is mental and emotional disturbance, and
the psychic feelings are all astir.

This is where messages of a purely psychic
origin can go wrong. You may be dismayed, not
realising that the distortion is the result of your
own inner disturbances. But you will realise that
disappointments of this nature are ultimately

good because they test the sincerity and staying power of the aspirant. If he is not earnestly treading the path, he fails to progress; but if he is true to himself he is not dismayed but keeps on striving for spiritual truth and learns how to discipline himself. When he has become dispassionate, calm and tranquil, he hears at last the inner voice. How does he hear? The innermost soul knows in a flash such an interchange of spiritual power from God, the Source of its being, that it can afterwards say in the face of all unbelief, 'I know because quite truly I have heard the voice of God speak. Nothing can ever shake or alter me after this experience.'

As the soul learns to overcome its turbulent emotions, to live tranquilly, kindly, lovingly, the physical body housing the soul should, as a result become in due time healthy and indeed perfect. We may touch upon rather a sensitive spot here because many people suffer more or less from ill health; their body is rarely the perfect expression of the Christ within. But how many people realise that undisciplined and uncontrolled emotions disturb their bloodstream and glandular system, and that this eventually produces minor, and later perhaps major, ailments? Of course this should not happen; after the Water Initiation has been passed, the soul can live calmly, patiently and happily day by day, unperturbed and undisturbed, reflecting only the heavenly, the true conditions of the God-life. In course of time it will be able to express through the body its own perfect wholeness or healthfulness.

So if you are at present sick in body or mind, take heart from what we say, and try to understand, try to absorb this one simple truth; and know that there is always a tomorrow, always a fresh opportunity waiting. Faithfully endeavour to attune all your higher bodies harmoniously to the spiritual law, and presently there will be re-created for you a new and perfect body, reborn from the harmony of the Christ within.

3

The Water Initiation

(II)

Sometimes when we open our hearts to the Great Spirit, the all-enfolding Love, Wisdom and Power, we pray that we may come into the Light of the Son, that we may lay down our burdens and come into God's heaven. But to lay down a burden does not mean to shed responsibility, for responsibility, if looked at in the right way, should not be a burden but rather an opportunity or even a joy; because while we are tested by our responsibilities we also earn them, and as the soul matures it becomes capable of undertaking more important tasks. If you could but realise, your responsibilities are also your opportunities for service.

Some people try to rid themselves of their responsibilities, and others take on unnecessary burdens and regard them as responsibilities. But we must learn to discriminate between the two. Do not the burdens and cares which weigh us down exist because we ourselves are in darkness, and do not understand the love, the power or the wisdom of God? Everything in life can become a burden instead of being part of that joy which our life should be. So when we say, 'Let us lay down our burdens,' the words really mean the laying down of unnecessary fears, anxieties and tortures which come through the soul's conflict with others, and with the conditions of its own life. When a man can see where he is going, when he has realised the power, the love and the wisdom of God, he carries his burdens no longer. We must therefore learn more about these attributes of God, for when we really understand the spiritual life we are filled with light, freedom and joy.

To illustrate this for yourselves, for one moment set aside all material things, and seek to enter into tranquillity and peace. As soon as you reach this state, your burdens begin to fall away, because you have entered into an *illumined* consciousness. When you know God, your soul will be filled with the radiance of God, it will be 'anointed,' and you will be able to meet all the situations of everyday life with complete tranquillity. We speak of this because, where the Bible describes the anointing of Jesus, it means that Jesus the mortal man, Jesus the prophet, Jesus the teacher, was anointed by the spirit of Christ entering into or taking possession of him at that moment.

We have previously discussed the baptism and explained that the experiences of Jesus the

Master are identical with the experiences through which every human soul will eventually pass. We shall try presently to compare these with some of your own soul-experiences and with those of every soul endeavouring to tread the path.

In course of time we shall all have to undergo four main initiations: every human soul reincarnates according to its needs, and each mortal life offers the soul its opportunity to undergo one or other of these four initiations.

At the moment we are still concerned with the Water Initiation, appertaining to the soul's desires, feelings or emotions—the psyche. This initiation is indeed one with which all those sensitive enough to touch the psychic realms are faced, and lies before all souls striving to overcome desire within their nature. Desire can manifest on every plane of man's being—physical, mental and spiritual; and the work of the candidate is not necessarily to erase but to gain full control over these feelings, emotions, and desires.

We are told that Jesus was called to the River Jordan to be baptised. Even today certain religious sects believe that by total immersion of the body in water something tangible happens to the soul. This may be true; but baptism really means that cleansing and purification which takes place when the soul feels 'called to Jordan,' or to the 'place of true repentance,' when the soul feels at last that it must find God. The human soul of Jesus, which was now age-old, already knew consciously many of these truths. But as we have said before, his whole life was pointing the way for all men to follow; every man will have to face the same tests. Although, if he has been previously tested in former lives he will remember, not in the mind but in the deeper self, and will be strong; and his subsequent initiations will therefore be simpler.

We are told that at Jordan Jesus heard the voice of God saying, '*This is my beloved Son in whom I am well pleased.*' You too may at some time have had some wonderful spiritual experience which has raised you to a state of joy and ecstasy. Perhaps this has come to you in the form of an actual communication with some loved one who has passed on, or during a religious service, or when listening to beautiful music—some outstanding, uplifting experience which has quickened you to recognise the presence and the glory of God. 'How wonderful are the ways of the spirit! How glorious is God!' you cry. Emotion overwhelms you. You feel that you have at last found your salvation.

The soul when thus deeply moved has literally heard the voice of God, and believes that it will never again look back. Such feelings are right and good at the time. But something comes after: when these wonders have been seen and heard, the testing follows. Everyone goes through this testing; indeed after the first arising of the spirit a whole series of tests awaits every soul on its path.

When this testing comes, some become disillusioned and think that all they believed to be true is wrong. But others are not so easily shaken, and though they may be perplexed and puzzled, they hold fast to the belief that they have both seen and heard the truth. They keep on keeping on.

Others again become disappointed with those they contact as they go about the world. People are only too ready to say, 'Well, fancy So-and-So, while professing religion, behaving like that!'— alas, forgetting that their companion is walking the selfsame path as they are and needs brotherhood, understanding and sympathy when he fails. 'Judge not that ye be not judged.' Indeed, we dare not judge anyone. While our brother may fall below our standard sometimes, so do we also fall. What treatment shall *we* expect when our turn comes? Think what it would mean to us were our brother to come to us then and say, 'Never mind; let us forget what happened. Let me help you to rise, brother, and carry on.'

Jesus, having received the call, we are told, went away into the wilderness. All aspirants, after hearing a similar call, have to return to take up their mortal life again and wander in the wilderness of the world. They want to be good, they try to hold fast to God and to the vision they have seen; but the world is so difficult and people are so difficult, and the aspirant is apt to look with despair at his particular part of the wilderness. The mists and illusions of the material world befog him. Nevertheless he is there to learn to hold fast to the Christ within himself. Only when this Christ power becomes established within can the candidate be called anointed.

Try not to think in terms of days, weeks or years, or about any particular period of time, but rather in terms of many incarnations; the way of the spirit is very sure, and slow and mysterious. Tests can be long continued, for the soul is intended to become very resolute in itself, very firmly established in the light of the Spirit. It has to turn continually inwards to the strength of its own inner spirit, of the Christ within. At every twist of the road, before every difficulty and problem confronting it, the soul must learn to hold fast to that inner light.

Jesus wandered in the wilderness for *forty* days. The Israelites dwelt for *forty* years in the wilderness. There are many references in the Bible to the number 'forty.' We think that use of this number originates from the period that a babe is carried in its mother's womb, roughly forty weeks; 'forty' therefore symbolises a time of confinement and limitation. The soul, after hearing the voice of God saying, 'This is my beloved Son,' must needs go through tests and trials arising out of its own limitation. If you have once seen heaven revealed, if only for a moment, and heard the voice of the spirit, you will understand. So great is the wonder that many people complain afterwards, 'Why have I to linger on in this old body? I wish I could be set free from it for ever,' not realising that they would not be out of their particular wood even then. Far from it! All is not glory in the spirit world unless a soul has the light shining within itself. All will depend on the quality of that soul, upon its present-day reactions when it faces up to conditions which seem very hard to bear, or is being tempted by Satan—meaning by Saturn, the planet which brings limitation. Yet you may be thankful for the influence of Saturn, for through the limitations and testings which it brings the soul grows strong and rich.

Let us read and ponder over the three temptations of Jesus, and try to associate them with our own personal experience, seeing how far they offer an explanation.

Then was Jesus led up of the Spirit into the wilderness, to be tempted of the devil. And when he had fasted forty days and forty nights, he was afterward an hungred. And when the tempter came to him, he said, If thou be the Son of God, command that these stones be made bread. But he answered and said, It is written, Man shall not live by bread alone, but by every word that proceedeth out of the mouth of God. (Matthew iv, 1-4.)

'*He was afterward an hungred.*' The body of Jesus, we learn, after this fast of forty days longed for food. This is, of course, but one interpretation, and indicates the temptation which can assail every soul which has gained power to perform miracles for its own satisfaction—but this the Christ or the true man will never do. However great his capacity, he will never use it for himself. But another interpretation is that when the soul has once seen the light, it longs for physical manifestation. People who are seeking the spirit world say, 'If only I could hear the actual voice of my loved one with my own ears, or see the materialised form with my own eyes, or really touch him, I should be satisfied ever after.' That is another method of trying to turn stones into bread. But even then the Christ within says, 'No, man should not live for physical manifestation alone, but by the Word of God, the spirit of God, by his inner knowledge of God.' The aspirant must deny any promptings to use the Christ power, the power of God, in order to satisfy himself.

The soul on the path should remain un-perturbed by any of these hammerings of the lower self. For it needs only to realise the light of God and hold fast to that inner knowledge, that inner light. It wants no outward manifestations. Yet to some these are a big temptation. Fasting, bodily purification will help, and are good if they also imply that the mind becomes clean and wholesome. Nevertheless it is not so much what a person eats as what he thinks, what he is in his inner self that purifies him. Let him by all means abstain from things which are unclean, by which we mean that which is innately unholy, unhealthy, unworthy. Fasting really means living in a state of purity. Of course, when a man's mind and soul grow pure because they have learned to abstain, his physical body no longer desires to eat anything which savours of cruelty, which is surely unholy and unhealthy.

Then the devil taketh him up into the holy city, and setteth him on a pinnacle of the temple, and saith unto him, If thou be the Son of God, cast thyself down: for it is written, He shall give his angels charge concerning thee: and in their hands they shall bear thee up, lest at any time thou dash thy foot against a stone. Jesus saith unto him, It is written again, Thou shalt not tempt the Lord thy God. (Matthew iv, 5-7.)

Notice that 'the devil taketh him up into the holy city,' the city of Jerusalem, to tempt him. Jerusalem means a centre of peace. When the soul enters 'Jerusalem' it means that it has found the place of peace. Yet if it is too sure of itself, the tempter within says, 'Why should I need to depend on God for everything? I can now do anything I like, having passed my test, my initiation. Now I can remain here indefinitely. No harm can befall my body or my soul. At last I am safe. Why then should I still continue to discipline myself?' You know the kind of argument which goes on in the soul, particularly after it has travelled a little way on the path? Then the Christ within arises and says, 'You must continue to strive after the perfect way, continue to be true to Me; beware of breaking the spiritual laws of God. You must not tempt the Lord your God.' This particular temptation originates from pride, in which there is a degree of ignorance.

There is also another interpretation. Some people are inclined to use their spiritual knowledge for their own ends, thinking that by sending out a sufficiently powerful thought they can attract anything they like to themselves—which is true. Send out a thought charged with occult power and you can draw material things to you. The initiate has to overcome this particular temptation. He must depend purely and simply upon the spirit of God, saying, 'Thy will, O God, not mine!' This really means surrender to the Divine Spirit, so that the soul does not try to use spiritual power to gain anything for itself, but lives sweetly and purely in the Christ light.

c

Again, the devil taketh him up into an exceeding high mountain, and sheweth him all the kingdoms of the world, and the glory of them; and saith unto him, All these things will I give thee, if thou wilt fall down and worship me. Then saith Jesus unto him, Get thee hence, Satan: for it is written, Thou shalt worship the Lord thy God, and him only shalt thou serve. Then the devil leaveth him, and behold, angels came and ministered unto him. (Matthew iv, 8-11.)

Many successful people—the good, religious people as well as the materially-minded—are tempted to believe that their success is entirely due to themselves. They think how clever they are! They forget that without the help and blessing of God nothing can ever be accomplished. Not through man alone but by the will of God do conditions arise in a human life destined to give the soul opportunities to serve God. Many worldly people become intoxicated with their own material success, and this can also happen on the spiritual path. People can become charged with spiritual pride, inwardly thinking how good they are and how nice they are to know! They have indeed been carried up into a high mountain. When the soul is thus raised, the tempter, which is the lower self, now whispers, 'How wonderful I am! It is *I* who have attained this spiritual height. *I* have made this great progress—all by myself!' But the soul who would triumph over these three temptations must know that whatever it achieves spiritually, it is of itself nothing and can do nothing; and that all the good that is in it is of God.

These temptations shrewdly come to test how strong is Christ within. For Christ speaking and acting in the soul is humble, pure, loving and gentle, ever meek and kind, wishing no evil and knowing no wrong, keeping on and on labouring in humility and love, and therefore growing very strong. This, then, is the purpose of Saturn or Satan, limiting and tempting us in our wilderness, to teach us to depend upon the gentle Christ within. Whatever your problem, whatever your hardship or difficulty—turn within; you will surely find your answer. Light will be shed upon your path. Have courage to face the truth, and you will then pass the Water Initiation, and will become firmly established as an initiate, as a master of the water element, the psychic, the emotional element in yourself. You can then create your heaven upon earth.

Seek God first—only God. As you seek you shall find.

4

The Proof in Life

We have dealt with the three particular temptations which every aspirant for the Water Initiation will have to undergo, and having triumphed over them, return to his appointed place in life. There he is filled with the power of the spirit and desire to preach the gospel, to share with others the truth that he has found. But *how* does the soul preach this wonderful gospel of truth? Already there are many, many people who by writing and talking are endeavouring to induce others to accept their beliefs. But truth is of the spirit, and cannot be conveyed by words alone. The initiate has to become a power in daily life, so that without preaching and often without even speaking, but by the emanation of his soul he teaches the gospel of truth, conveying truth to his fellow beings by the measure of the Christ spirit within him. 'By their fruits ye shall know them.' This means by the manifestation of the spirit of Christ, the radiance given forth by the soul. From some people you can receive a great deal without a word being spoken. Such individuals are often retiring and are certainly humble, gentle and tender with their fellows, but have within them the power of the spirit which they are continually giving out to heal the sick in mind and body, to comfort the mourner and raise those who are downcast in spirit.

They are also giving true riches to the poor. '*Blessed are the poor in spirit,*' Jesus said. Who are these poor in spirit? They are those who have reached a stage in their spiritual development where they are ready both to receive and absorb truth and light from an initiate. Yet there are many, many souls who are not yet ready; who scoff at spiritual truth and are interested only in worldly things, and who, because they are arrogant and do not want to hear, have not yet earned the title 'poor in spirit.' The poor in spirit are able to recognise God, they see God shining through the initiate. The initiate is ever radiating true power, spiritual light, Christ-likeness; and the 'poor in spirit' are souls ready to absorb his radiance. Blessed are they because they are found waiting.

We think that there are a great many people today who have unknowingly reached the stage of being 'poor in spirit.' If so, they have all a great work before them, not necessarily to be accomplished by teaching or preaching from a platform or pulpit, but by putting the power of Christ into their everyday life. With Christ anything can be accomplished; the mistake that so many people make is to depend on their own power. For the secret is to enter the heart-chamber, the inner self, the place of tranquillity and stillness, and there pray; in other words, to stand on one side and let the God-power work through the medium of the body, mind and soul. Then there is nothing that cannot be accomplished, because whatever is done is to the glory of God. Any soul able to commune with God is ready to manifest God.

A number of the Master's miracles were concerned with the healing of the blind. The 'blind' represent those who lack understanding of spiritual truth. While their souls yearn for love they cannot feel it, they cannot give it. They are unaware of the invisible worlds of great beauty and radiance about them, or that they themselves live in a world which, rightly viewed, is a world of spiritual glory. What wonderful work it is to be able to open the eyes of those who dwell in darkness and show them that there is no death, and there need never be separation even when the spirit of their beloved quits his physical body for another world! This is the work of those who have passed the Water Initiation, those who have controlled their psychic forces and who are able to see into the other worlds, and convey their vision of truth to their fellows.

Yet if a soul is not ready to learn, no power on earth will make it ready. It is all a question of the awakening or awareness of the person concerned. 'To everything there is a season, and a time to every purpose under the heaven.' Once any person has earned the right to know spiritual truth, his teacher will surely be forthcoming. Sometimes men and women become excited and long to meet a Master in the flesh. They are usually disappointed. But when they have at last reached the point where they are able to recognise a Master, then the Master will manifest. They themselves will by then have created the necessary conditions in which to receive from the Master the illumination, teaching, comfort and help they require, in readiness for the next step on the path. It is a great work to restore sight to the blind; or, in other words, to be able to illumine them through the power of the Christ spirit within.

The inner self of man can become so powerful and so Christ-like that it conveys healing, teaching, blessing. The effect of this cannot be superficial and transient, for it comes from God Himself within the soul and is therefore eternal and infinite. Within every soul God dwells, although there are many layers to be peeled off before His light can shine forth. Those who are a little more advanced than others can indeed sometimes help in the casting off of some of these outer coverings.

5

The Air Initiation

(I)

It has been said that dispassion is one of the most difficult lessons for the neophyte to learn. It is so very easy for him to allow himself to become emotionally upset by contact with inharmonious conditions or people. But as the Christ light within grows stronger it teaches the neophyte to control passion and emotion, to keep them stilled and in their right place, so that they no longer storm through his soul, upsetting and shattering him.

So we learn through the Water Initiation the meaning of becoming still, so that the tranquil waters of the soul may reflect God, whatever the circumstances of life. But a clear distinction must be made between indifference and lethargy, and that tranquillity and calmness based on strength, when a clear perspective has been attained and the soul is under the direction of the Master, the Christ.

After the Water Initiation comes the Air Initiation. We have said that the four initiations— Water, Air, Fire, Earth—are not necessarily taken separately. Indeed, frequently the neophyte may be preparing for all four initiations during one span of life on earth. Certainly, as soon as ever he enters upon the spiritual path he will begin to be tried, tested and trained. During certain periods his soul may respond more readily to one of these four, in which element he may mainly work. Here we are taking the initiations separately mainly for the sake of clarity, and to help you better to understand what is happening when you come up against them in your human relationships.

As Water is symbolic of the *emotional* nature of man, so Air is of his *mental* nature. The Air element is that of the mind. We shall find that the human mind is as difficult to understand and handle as the emotions; and that just as a man's uncontrolled emotions obstruct the development and progress of his soul, so also can his lower mind.

The object of the Air Initiation is that the higher mind (remember that there are two aspects of the mind) should take possession and become the ruler of the neophyte's thoughts. His thoughts must become spiritually pure so that the mind can receive and the life become adjusted to spiritual truth—and then there is no longer conflict between the higher and the lower mind. For instance, the soul may at one time undergo a glorious and uplifting experience, and the indwelling truth in the man will assure him that his soul has indeed been caught up to heaven. But afterwards his soul has to return again to earth to be assailed by doubts, fears and questions. The lower mind thus becomes the tempter, doing all it can to refute, to confuse, or even to overshadow and overpower the higher mind. The higher mind receives the inspiration, the in-breathing of the *air* of God, but it needs to be continually fortified against the arguments of the lower mind. The neophyte has to train himself to be loyal and true, to resist staunchly any such arguments, knowing that they are spoken only by the mind of earth; he has to learn both to discern this fact, and put this earthly mind back in its correct place!

In the course of preparation for the Air Initiation these testings will be frequent, as most of you are already aware; but we would guide and help you to be very strong and to allow your intuition or your higher mind at all times to be master of the earthly mind. The former will never mislead. If you will be true to this higher mind you will obtain a wise answer to any of your problems.

It is said that Mercury is the messenger of the gods. It is also said that Mercury is the ruler of the fifth world, or sphere of the higher mind, and proceeds from higher spheres to bring truth to man. Mercury also rules the zodiacal sign of Gemini. The symbol of Gemini, as you know, is the 'heavenly twins,' or the 'two pillars.' These are the two pillars between which the soul has to pass into the temple of initiation. Shall we call one of these pillars the higher mind (which is situated at the back of the head), and the other the frontal mind, the intellect or mind of earth? In this Air Initiation the neophyte has to learn true discernment in order to pass between the pillars of the higher and the lower mind. There must be perfect accord between the two. Then he achieves the Air Initiation.

You all experience the conflict between these two minds, these two 'selves.' Probably your main difficulty will be to refute the telling arguments of the worldly mind, for they sound so sane and practical; but it is vitally important for the mind of earth to be controlled by the mind of the intuition, the mind of Christ, the mind of the spirit.

The lower mind is largely of the body, and so inherits all the racial instincts and memories transmitted to the body; it has all the attributes of death. It fears the higher mind, and would destroy the Christ in man. The story of the trial of Jesus tells how the Pharisees, or those filled with selfishness, pride and arrogance—all qualities of the lower mind—sought to kill Christ, the higher mind, because Christ stood in their way. The story of Joseph and his brethren has much the same meaning. But as man evolves and progresses, his higher mind will employ the mind of earth for the benefit of man, instead of the latter trying to obliterate the higher mind. The initiate has to learn balance—that is, the lesson of equilibrium, the balancing of opposites.

Many a miracle and parable in the Bible specially refers to this Air Initiation. There is one where a man's right hand, here symbolic of the higher mind, had become withered and useless. The Master called forth the power of the higher mind in the man and restored the withered arm. Afterwards Jesus was chided by the Jews for healing on the Sabbath Day. Now the Sabbath Day (Saturn's Day) by interpretation means the day of meditation and quiet contemplation of the works of God. Saturn, it is said, is a strict master and will allow no slipshod methods. No soul can pass through the ring of Saturn to enter the temple of heaven until it has passed the fine tests which Saturn sets. In other words, in true meditation the soul stands before the judgment bar, and cannot get away with anything but truth. This is why Saturn is called the 'ring-pass-me-not.' Nevertheless Saturn can be considered as man's greatest friend. That is perhaps why Jesus chose the Jewish Sabbath or Saturn's Day upon which to heal this withered higher mind and bring it again into action.

Another parable tells how on a Sabbath Day the disciples plucked the ears of corn and rubbed them in their hands, extracting and eating the good grain and letting the chaff blow away. Here the chaff represents the lower mind. The disciples under the tuition of their Master were able to extract truth through their higher mind, and so learned discernment and discrimination between the higher and the lower mind. All the conflict existing in the world arises between these two aspects, these two pillars; thus you will see how vitally important it is to discern the difference between the promptings of the lower and the higher mind, and to think right thoughts. It is useless a man striving to make the outer world a better place until his innermost thoughts are true, pure and heavenly. Saints and seers and prophets and teachers of all time have learned the secret of right thought, good thought, God thought, and they have not worried about anything else. They *become* within themselves; they are themselves lights in a world of darkness. The world may not recognise them; but always they radiate positive and loving thoughts, kind, gentle and compassionate thoughts, ever helping to sow more seeds of right thought in the world of men. All things originate from thought. God's thought created all things. All physical form is a manifestation of thought. Your world today manifests the result either of its good or evil thinking, because thought eventually creates form in matter.

We are on the cusp of the Aquarian Age, the age both of the spirit and of the mind. If the higher mind does not control the lower, then chaos and destruction will ensue. Nevertheless the higher mind is already everywhere manifesting itself. Even in material affairs men and women are beginning to think how to make the world a better place, how to improve the conditions of the down-trodden. These are all good thoughts and come because the higher mind is being stimulated. Those of you who are striving after spiritual truth must learn continually to project from your heart and your higher mind thoughts of goodwill, brotherhood and love. Always see good in the ascendant, even if it appears comparatively infinitesimal. See good arising no matter what the situation may be. Always project the light of Christ from your soul. Let your thoughts of love and goodwill be continually broadcast upon the ether. You can never know how great will be your service. Let your higher mind dominate your life, and you will help many others along their path back to God.

6

The Air Initiation

(II)

God is all wisdom and love and gives to us everything we need; but it is not easy for you to have complete confidence in this divine providence, particularly when events do not unfold as you would like them to do. Delay is one of the trials which beset most aspirants on the path, because when the soul has seen how wonderful life may be, it longs to bring the same vision to all people; feeling sure that if its life were different, if some of its handicaps were removed, if only the right opportunities would come along, then at last it could render that help to humanity which it so longs to give. This period of waiting and testing is most difficult for the soul to accept with patience, because at such times the soul believes it knows best, only wishing that other people would be more gracious and receptive.

My brethren, let us at this moment become still in mind and spirit, and in imagination let us enter into the temple of God...... Now, as we do so, we become conscious of its radiance, and of the countless souls gathered to worship. We

behold the altar blazing with light; we behold the
Divine Master ministering to all creation at that
altar. An inward voice tells us that we too are
come to receive our measure of that holy ministra-
tion, and in the degree that we are able to receive
and absorb His divine essence (the bread and wine)
into our hearts, we become blessed with inner
peace. We have surrendered all cares, frets and
fevers of the lower mind, for as we meditate before
the Divine Presence we know that all is well, that
God is all wisdom and His ways are those of an
ever-loving parent, patient, forgiving, perfect and
true. An earthly parent may believe he truly
loves, and yet will often over-indulge his child,
mistaking his own indulgence for love; but the
Heavenly Father loves perfectly, and often His
wiser love causes Him to withhold that which the
child would grasp at and hold. Now we catch a
glimpse of the dispassionate mind, the higher
mind at work. In this moment of revelation we
are able to comprehend a Love which both gives
and withholds—a Mind which never hurries because it is completely sure of the outworking of
divine laws ordained to bring to the child of earth
the blessing of full realisation of itself and of the
fullness of God's providence.

We have said of the Air Initiation that it
brings recognition of and discrimination between

the two minds of man—the earthly mind, and the mind of Christ, the higher or the heavenly mind. We have dwelt on the testing and the resultant conflict between these two. You know well how the so-called reason can argue against the higher mind. How reasonable seem those arguments advanced by the lower mind, which tell us why we should never let ourselves become too sentimental or idealistic; why we should always be practical and think first of our own well-being. Yet the mind of Christ in us reveals another, a better way of life; and whilst the higher mind prevails when we are in the temple of the spirit, yet it knows well that when the man goes back to the world to face all the problems of life, his so-called reason is likely to overpower him again for the time being. The task in hand is for the soul to become so strong in the Christ spirit that the higher mind rules every detail, and life is controlled and directed not by this so-called reason but by inspiration.

You will ask how this may be achieved. The way is by continual meditation; not only in times of quiet, but throughout your day. Go about your tasks always conscious of your higher self as a background to your actions, of your higher mind operating from the back of your brain; thus in time the higher mind will become an active part of you, directing every thought and action so that

D

the mind of earth automatically, instantly, obeys. The secret is to keep very tranquil and control the emotions. This is why the first degree entails control of the emotional body—control of the emotions of passion, fear, depression and anger. This means continual discipline; but if man refuses to discipline himself, then God has to discipline him perhaps through poverty, hunger, sorrow or persecution. If he allows the will of God within to discipline him, then attainment can be achieved quickly. You may think it is easier to keep on jogging along and not to try to hurry your soul's evolution. But if you know the Promised Land is very near and by making an effort you can get there quickly, is it not better to make that effort, however hard it may be, than to have to endure the petty sufferings of a rebellious soul over a long period?

God is all love. His ways are gentle and kind; and if the man is willing to open to the love of God he will be filled with all blessings. But if he is rebellious and blind, then inevitably he suffers. The soul must acquire all the qualities of the Christ mind—meekness, acceptance, humility, peace— but not necessarily by the hard way! It can, if it will, learn much through happiness and joy, beauty and plenty. However, if the lessons are not learnt, then these things are taken away and the soul learns through lack of them.

Throughout the Bible many references to these two minds will be found in symbolic form. We are told that Moses led the children of Israel into the wilderness for 'forty' years—a space of time symbolising a period of waiting for their birth into spiritual life, into a Promised Land of light and understanding. Although the people knew that they were being led towards this Promised Land, they grumbled and complained bitterly. Here we see the lower mind at work. We learn that because of their rebellion, neither Moses nor most of his followers crossed into the Promised Land. But their children entered in, led not by Moses but by Joshua. We interpret this to mean that Joshua was representative of the higher mind. You will remember that Moses was allowed to see the glories of that land from afar, but not to taste the richness of it. Is not that the way with us all? We wander for a long time in our particular wilderness, undergoing our personal testings, our course of preparation; and in due time we reach our Promised Land, or state of illumination where the higher mind comes into its own, and then tastes the fruits and enjoys the wonders of the heavenly places.

Some of you are already being trained in the art of meditation. You may not yet have reached the Promised Land but it is waiting, and in due time you will not only see but will actually enter in and enjoy the realisation of heavenly places and experience illumination of the higher mind.

We spoke before about the disciples plucking the ears of corn and rubbing them in their hands, so that the husks blew away and the grain was left. Even then the corn needed to be ground into flour before it could be baked into bread. The true disciple must rub away the useless husk, the material earthly things, but he is still left with the hard grains of corn which have to be pounded by the experience of many a life before they can become the living bread. The grinding of the corn means the working out in everyday life of the spiritual truths which the higher mind learns.

Elsewhere the Old Testament tells of twelve little loaves of shewbread which were kept in the temple. This brings to mind the twelve zodiacal experiences by which every soul learns while in incarnation, reincarnating again and yet again until it has accomplished what are symbolically 'the twelve labours of Hercules.' The twelve little loaves (or experiences) represent the sum total of human incarnation. Before they are taken into the temple they are sprinkled with incense— which means that man has to become meek enough to learn his lessons sweetly, and not in a harsh or resentful way. He must present his bread, the sum total of his incarnations, lovingly sprinkled with the sweet incense of humility so that it may be acceptable to God.

Many people, governed only by the mind of earth, say that the Sermon on the Mount is impractical in modern times. Yet the Sermon on the Mount is as true today as it was yesterday and will be for ever. In it Jesus gave to his disciples, who had by now passed the first degree and were in preparation for the second, certain inner principles or rules which have to be learned and applied before the soul can be fully initiated. He divided his discourse into two parts—first stating the four aspects or four tests which every initiate would have to face; and secondly outlining the four attitudes of mind in which the candidate must accept these tests.

Two statements in the Bible would appear to be contradictory. Both concern the Sermon on the Mount. One reads: '*He went up into a mountain . . . . . . and his disciples came unto him*' (Matthew v, 1); and the other reads: '*He came down with them and stood in the plain*' (Luke vi, 17). Yet the two can be reconciled; because the going up into the mountain means a rising in consciousness, when the soul enters into or functions in the higher mind. But Jesus, although he had attuned himself to an exalted state in order to receive truth, had also to come down to the plain, to descend to the level of the people in order to speak to them at their plane of understanding. So he described the things they would have to encounter, explaining that if they accepted their testing rightly they would be blessed.

The tests in themselves are not so important. It is the soul's *reaction* to them, the attitude of mind adopted, that really matters; because the higher mind must govern this reaction and never the lower. If the higher mind deals with life's problems, the soul will absorb the qualities of Christ—meekness, mercy, purity and peace. It will learn to be meek in adversity, and merciful to all; to be faithful in purity of life and thought, and to know absolute peace in surrender to God. Meekness, mercy, purity and peace are the four qualities which are essential to the soul seeking to pass the Air Initiation.

We often talk about 'sacrifice'—perhaps we use the word too much. Shall we not rather say 'surrender'? For the soul no longer thinks in terms of sacrifice when it has become gentle, merciful, pure and peaceful. With the attainment of these qualities the thought of sacrifice fades because the candidate has learned the lesson of divine love, and has reached such understanding and love for its brethren that its only real happiness lies in serving them.

So we might say that the Air Initiation brings home the lesson of brotherly service. The higher mind being triumphant enables the soul to serve out of pure love for its brethren. Having learned to practise brotherhood, it has entered into the outer courts of heaven, to consort with companions of its spirit, and receive illumination from Christ its Lord.

7

The Fire Initiation

Warmth in nearly every form originates from the sun. Yet there is a spiritual as well as a physical sun, for behind every physical form is the spirit which is part of God, and which brings that form into being; without the invisible or spirit sun pervading the sun above there would be no light or warmth to sustain man's world. And the spirit behind the sun is moreover identical with that spirit in you which you call 'love.'

Some people mistakenly believe that love is only a wayward feeling or an emotion. No: love is the first cause of all life. Love is light and heat and life itself. This is the supreme secret which the third initiation, known as the Fire Initiation, reveals to the soul.

We remind you again that the Water Initiation entails the control and the right use of man's emotions, and the Air Initiation the right use of the mental bodies or the mental abilities of man. Yet we find that the Air Initiation, which disciplines and trains the mind, can still leave the soul cold—let us say, as air remains chill while the sun is obscured. So we think of the mind also as being cold; for we know that intellectualism is cold and exacting, and because of this it cannot live. So the Air initiate turns to something which will bring him warmth and life. However brilliant the mind, unless it become infused with the love of God, all its works will gradually fade and die. It is the Fire Initiation which brings warmth and light and beauty into life. Those of you who have begun the practice of meditation have been taught to search for the spark of light within, the 'dot within the circle.' The interior of the circle may be dark, but at the centre point the light is shining. You learn to fix your mind upon that light as a first lesson in concentration.

Now many people, although they have learned to control their emotions and have disciplined and trained their minds, remain imprisoned, unable to live in the world of spirit. It is as if they were shut in a closed room, or in an iron box; and their constant heart-cry is, 'How can I become free? How can I see, live and move in a world of spirit? No matter how I struggle, I cannot break my bonds!' The reason for this state of bondage is that they are still striving through cold reason and logic to find their way out. This they will never do. Perhaps it sounds too homely when we say that the way to release yourself from bondage is through simple love; but this is the truth.

The Fire Initiation opens the third degree of

human consciousness. In his earliest stage man is unconscious; then he becomes a self-conscious being; and the third degree confers upon him a measure of divine consciousness. When this is attained, the man has become an initiate of the fire element. It should be understood that all these elements operate on every plane of man's being, from lowest earth to high in heaven. Love can be active on all planes. The lower man only becomes aware of love as a passion that sears, burns and consumes, but on the highest plane it creates and gives life.

How can you open the door to the divine life? Certainly not by overwork on the mental plane! First you must endeavour to *feel* within yourself the attributes of Christ the Son of God—the warmth of his love for humanity, his gentleness, humility, patience and peace of spirit. Attune yourself as far as you can to the spirit of the Son of God, the Lord Christ. Contemplate his nature, his brotherhood, his understanding. Dwell in his spirit. Let everything else go, as you enter into his consciousness. You will then find that this small point of light on which you concentrate will expand until it becomes a golden sun, bringing warmth and freedom. Then you enter into the land of warmth and light and life. When this occurs the vision which first opens to the young initiate is usually that of natural and rare beauty—

of flowers, trees, and birds, and living, shining waters; because, as the Spirit of God brought forth life on the earth in the beginning, so it brings forth life for you on the astral and the higher planes. Love creates beauty.

Those who have long neglected to love others find themselves in a state of darkness, chill loneliness and barrenness when they pass into the next world. *Love, and love alone, gives life.* That which endures in art, music, literature and religion has been infused with both human and divine love. Other works of man's brain tend to disintegrate and disappear because they lack this quality.

The demonstration of the surpassing power of love at the transfiguration is the finest, we think, ever recorded in the New Testament, although many other illustrations can be cited. In the Old Testament we read of the initiate Moses and the burning bush, and later of his ascending a mountain. Now 'going up into the mountain' means his being raised in consciousness; and in that state he became so illumined, so full of fire and light that when he descended to meet the children of Israel he had to veil his face. In another passage we read of the pillar of fire by which the Israelites were led out of their bondage —away from the flesh-pots of Egypt, from material things. Afterwards they had to wander in the wilderness for forty years. So it is with a man who has relinquished his material way of life; though released from bondage, he may still be wandering in the wilderness, and waiting to find entry into his Promised Land. The reference to the 'pillar of cloud by day and the pillar of fire by night' means the fire of love, the spiritual light, by which God reveals His divine presence to His chosen people.

In Exodus xxiv we read that Moses went up into the mount, and was in the mount for forty days and forty nights—'forty' meaning a period of gestation before the full birth or the full initiation; and that when Moses ascended the mount, fire descended upon him. This really means the rising of the creative fires throughout his whole being, a process sometimes described as fire running up the spine like lightning and illuminating the head. The dawn of cosmic consciousness means that the soul breaks its bonds and becomes united with the Universal Mind. When Moses came down from the mount he 'wist not that the skin of his face shone.' This also is the meaning of the halo around the heads of saints; their very flesh shines with light.

Now let us consider the story of the transfiguration of Jesus. You will remember that at the time of the baptism, of the Water Initiation, the voice from heaven cried, *'This is my beloved Son, in whom I am well pleased!'* But notice that God still withheld full authority at that time. At this Fire

Initiation He added, '*Hear ye him.*' It was this baptism of fire which finally authorised Jesus to speak and to serve his brethren in the Name and Power of God.

We read that when Jesus went up into the mountain—or remember, entered a higher state of consciousness—three disciples, Peter, James and John, accompanied him. On the higher plane with Jesus appeared two initiates, Elias and Moses. Now Peter, James and John (as here portrayed in the Gospels) stand for the three separate qualities of faith, hope and love; the three qualities which must govern the soul when about to undergo the Fire Initiation.

When you enter upon the path of spiritual service and development, the very first quality in which you are tested, and which you will have to be strengthened to hold fast to, is that of *faith*. However difficult things are, and even if all seem to have deserted you and you stand alone, you still have to keep your faith that all is well, that you are in the care of your Father. You must hold on to your faith that God has power to bring you through the valley of shadows, and that you are being wisely guided and led. You have also to keep your hope shining bright. Faith is an inward knowing that all is right and is working for your good; hope means an ever-growing confidence in God's wisdom, in the way you are being led. Above all, when these two qualities of faith and hope grow strong within, you have also to develop that state of glorious fire, called love, which illumines your heart and life as well as your countenance, so that light goes forth to others through your mind, through your emotions, your speech and every action. Through your whole being love flows out into the world, to touch those who are lifeless, those who are dead. Many spiritually dead people are walking your streets, particularly in the great cities, but when you have attained this Fire Initiation you will have power to bring these souls to life, power to send light to illumine their darkness, to heal their sick minds and bodies.

When the soul passes the Fire Initiation it undergoes a supreme experience which changes its whole life—as happened to Saul (later called Paul) on the road to Damascus, when a great light blinded him. It was a sudden illumination, a sudden overwhelming realisation of the reality of God's life and God's love.

In due time this will come to each one of you. The light will flood your being and all your gifts will be enhanced by the incoming of this divine fire, this magic, this creative power. This is the power that initiates use to perform what people call miracles, which acts not only upon the human mind and emotions, but on matter itself. Like the old alchemy it will transmute base metal into pure gold! A transmutation such as this is the aspiration, the ultimate goal of all brethren following the path, who seek earnestly, without thought of self, to serve their brother men. To love is to serve. Therefore we say, 'Cultivate the art of loving others and forget yourself!' Self-consciousness is a form of darkness. Your lower self must be put behind.

Let us consider the symbol of a lighted candle; the wick burns brightly and little by little the wax around that flame dissolves and burns away. In a like manner the flame of divine love by degrees consumes the lower self; it is transmuted and transformed. Love transforms life, removing all that is ugly and unwanted. The transmuting power of love is the magical secret of the initiate's life. When this love fills the heart, the heart centre glows with divine fire and radiates like the sun, and can be seen in the breast of all who have passed the Fire Initiation.

8

The Earth Initiation

We now turn to the last of the four initiations—the Earth Initiation. Some believe that the Fire Initiation should be thought of as final, because in it we become consciously aware of the Divine Fire. But Saul, after he had been struck by the blinding light, had still to prove himself, had still to be tested for his final initiation.

The Earth Initiation is necessary because even after the soul has received divine illumination, even after it has been caught up into the heavens and seen the vision glorious, it has to learn *to use* the power of the Divine Fire in order to control physical matter wisely and rightly. This is what some call the secret magic. You have heard stories of the Masters being able to perform what the world calls miracles; they can pass matter through matter, and can traverse great distances in a flash of time; they can produce food to feed the hungry, and can actually raise the so-called dead! Millions still doubt whether miracles such as these have ever actually happened. This is only because the ordinary mind cannot understand the process involved. We were once asked: 'If the

Masters are really able to feed the hungry whenever they desire, why don't they feed starving children in our midst?' A very understandable question! The Masters do not miraculously produce food for the starving because that would mean interfering with men's karma. Men, women and children too are evolving towards spiritual emancipation through their life experiences, and no Master, no guide, and not even an angel can do the work of regeneration for any other soul. Everyone must tread his appointed path from birth onwards, until the soul by its own aspiration and endeavour, frees itself from the bondage of its lower nature and its prison-house of matter. The whole purpose of life is that every soul on earth may develop God powers, and in time become a true son or daughter of a living, loving God—not a God seated on a throne in a far-away heaven, but Whose life and essence permeate every atom of His creation and every vibration of man's inner being.

In the Earth Initiation each individual soul has to learn that all substance is God; that everything which seems solid matter is really charged with divine energy and light. You are all enslaved in matter, enslaved by the earthly conditions which encompass you. The Earth Initiation teaches the soul how to free itself from the bondage of matter by a process of surrender which

E

can be likened to crucifixion and death. But an Earth initiate knows that he cannot die, for there is no such thing as death. No matter how stoutly a man believes that death ends all, and even persuades himself that he wants to die, he must still live on. The candidate for Earth Initiation has not merely to accept this truth of continuing existence but to realise it within his very being— that neither his soul nor his body can ever die. True, a body seems wholly empty and dead when its soul and spirit withdraw, unable longer to sustain the body's burden and inharmony; but its casting off is only like the shedding of the serpent's skin. True also, that body will afterwards disintegrate, and all its particles scatter; but these particles will continue to exist in another form, much as the soul still continues apart from the body, and eventually after a preliminary cleansing returns to its true home, which is in a *body of light*.

But more than this, if you could once realise that your physical body can be healed and protected against all harm by a shield of light, and that within you burns the Divine Fire of life; if you could live always conscious of this light, you would find that the very atoms of your body would gradually become etherealised. Then you would live for evermore in a body of light, although it is true that this new body of light will make little impression on people who are still imprisoned in matter, shut away from the light like prisoners bolted and barred in a dark cell.

What then brings about this change in the physical matter of your body? It is the action of the Divine Fire of love awakened by the voice of God within man's innermost heart. Some would call this voice the 'I AM' speaking—but you must learn to distinguish between the promptings of the personal 'I' which is of the earth, and the divine 'I AM,' the voice of the living God—the voice divine, pure, humble, lowly, gentle, patient, kindly—the voice of Christ, the only begotten of the Father.

What does 'only begotten' mean? The term does not suggest any form of physical parentage but union of the Father-Mother God in the heavens. Before the earth was created—I AM! This 'I AM' is the living and universal Christ, born deep in the cave of the heart in every man (as in the lowly stable at Bethlehem, and come to birth among the lowliest and humblest of God's creatures). The voice of the 'I AM' in every heart leads man, the Son of God, through pain and crucifixion of earth into eventual inheritance of a pure body of light in a world of light.

We are not theorising, we are speaking of scientific truth; for your scientists already know that matter is not so solid as men were wont to think, and that something exists which is more real, more potent than material force and energy, which in the very core of the atom is responsible for the construction of matter. This something is spiritual substance and energy.

After the Earth Initiation the candidate will be able to see that what he had formerly thought to be solid earth substance is not solid at all; and that the power, capable of quickening the vibrations of matter to that point where it becomes invisible to ordinary sight, is the Divine Fire or light of Christ.

Think along these lines and try to realise that your true state of embodiment is in the eternal light. If you cannot contact the light during meditation it is because the lower self still imprisons you. If you will persevere in seeking the 'I AM,' which is deeply buried in your innermost heart, you will gradually become aware of this inner spark of light. As development proceeds you will at times find yourself enveloped in a golden radiance, and you will know the meaning of the words, 'We live and move and have our being in God.' God is our light; in Him only do we truly live, and without Him we have no real life at all.

So you will see that after the Fire Initiation, where the soul becomes aware of the light, the next stage must be for the soul to learn to make use of the light, and through its power to gain dominion over physical matter and all the lower or intractable elements of its own being and outer environment. This is the way which every soul will some day tread. The story of the crucifixion is universal to all men, in that it explains the entire process of the Earth Initiation. Every ordinary man will in time become a candidate for initiation and will go through a form of crucifixion of mind, soul or body; will suffer the pain of crucifixion, and because of this know the meaning of the resurrection and ascension of Christ. This great surrender or crucifixion applies not only to individuals but also to nations, to entire races of men and indeed to whole worlds. All mankind must follow the same path. Mankind must suffer in darkness and blindness until of its own desire it surrenders self-will and becomes identified with the will of God. This will of God working out in individual and nation alike manifests as love, goodwill, brotherhood, justice, truth and peace.

Let us review the events of the crucifixion, from which we can learn that the light, the Divine Fire, was already burning in the soul of Jesus, but he, the man, had still to go through his final initiation, and as part of that great initiation he was betrayed. So also will every soul at some time know the meaning of betrayal, of being cruelly and unjustly treated. When this happens man's lower self rises in indignation and demands justice. The Earth Initiation, however, teaches the soul that it is never right to hit back at anyone, and that the only way for the initiate is to forgive. Did not Jesus pray, 'Father, forgive them; for they know not what they do'? The awakened soul of Jesus knew that if those who tortured and betrayed him fully realised the purport of their actions, they could not have done these things. For indeed, man can never wilfully betray or torture another once he understands the full implications of his act, or the debt that he incurs. The heart-cry of the initiate is ever this, 'Father, forgive them; for they know not what they do!'

Let us consider another incident which occurred during the hours of crucifixion, when Jesus called upon John and Mary standing at the foot of the cross, saying to John, 'Behold thy mother!'—while to Mary he said, 'Woman, behold thy son!' The 'woman' here is a symbol of the soul; 'John,' of the divine spirit; and the deeper meaning of the incident is that the soul and the divine spirit of Jesus were at that moment merging, embracing, being eternally united. Life for man on earth is not finished or complete until this divine union—or as the Hermetic philosophers say, this 'mystical marriage'—has taken place. The meaning is the same as in another parable, when the soul, portrayed by the wise virgins who had made ready, went forth to meet the bridegroom.

Later upon the cross Jesus cried, 'I thirst!' According to the scriptures, the soldiers in attendance gave him vinegar and gall to drink—a bitter, bitter draught. But his thirst was not of the earth; his thirsting soul at that moment was calling upon the spiritual powers for succour. Nothing else could give him that for which he craved.

We are told that at his last moments on the cross Jesus cried out, '*My God, my God, why hast Thou forsaken me?*' Again the soul was calling upon God, because the power of the lower self upon which men usually depend was failing and departing. After his Earth Initiation man must solely rely upon the light and the glory of God. God alone is man's stay and salvation.

Then came the cry from Jesus: 'It is finished!' This meant that he had finally overcome and was wholly master of the lower self. The lower self was silenced, dead. Think for a moment of the unending conflict between his two opposing selves which goes on throughout all the years of a man's many lives. At this supreme moment the spirit of Jesus was freed, released. His true self beheld the glory of his Father in heaven, and made the great surrender. Conflict had ceased. Had he not previously promised the thief on his right hand, 'Today shalt thou be with me in paradise'? These two thieves crucified with Jesus represent man's higher and his lower mind—in this story the lower mind is symbolised by the thief who was debarred from heaven, and the higher by the thief who went onward with the Christ.

Then said Jesus, 'Father, into Thy hands I commend my spirit'—and with these words went forth into the glory of the Father.

This was the complete and final triumph of Jesus; and this, brethren, is the final initiation for which the souls of all men are being prepared and which they will some day undergo. All will one day realise that they have always lived and had their being safe in God's life and love; that all their fears were empty, idle fears; and that the real purpose of their earth lives has been to teach them to realise their power of command over the four elements and over all matter, so that they could in the end rule as kings in the kingdom of eternal light.

The Resurrection and Ascension

We must refer briefly to the problems of time and space—that is, of dimensional time and space. When we say that there is no such thing as time on the spiritual planes of existence or indeed on earth, you will smile at us, because your clocks take their time from the sun and their 'hours' limit your whole conception of life. In spirit there is no such limitation, because all time is at this instant! At this very instant you and we are in eternity! All that was or ever will be is existing *now*. Thus you may, if you wish, go forward or backward in time. Your degree of realisation of the nature of eternity is all that limits you.

This may help you to grasp that here, now and always you are enfolded in the love of the great White Brotherhood; that you are encompassed by a vast company of unseen companions of your spirit, some of whom you may have known and loved in former earth lives, and whom you can meet again on the plane of pure spirit. Whenever you aspire to truth, you are in contact with the age-old companions of your spirit. This means that when you have undergone the discipline necessary to enable you to become an initiate, you will know how to raise yourself to them. The average man seldom thinks of his personal problems, anxieties, and even agonies as having any relation to his initiation; but every sorrow, every painful experience is helping your soul towards liberation and to realisation of the kingdom of heaven, and is therefore infinitely worthwhile.

Let us refer again briefly to the Earth Initiation; for by now you may have attained a degree of spiritual understanding of these matters and may even have glimpsed the spiritual realms and felt the presence of your guides, teachers or helpers. Yet at this point many people stop short: they know the power is available, is waiting for them, but only theoretically; when it comes to making use of this power, they fail to bring it through or allow it to overrule their daily selves. Here is the secret purpose of what is called the Earth Initiation.

We are told that after the crucifixion, the body of the Master lay in the grave for three days, and that during this period Jesus visited souls in hell. He associated himself with his brethren who were suffering. When you yourself have passed through something which seems to you like a crucifixion, cannot you more fully identify yourself with the sufferings of others? An initiate knows the reason for his crucifixion, but the souls whom the Master visited were in hell because they did not know the purpose of their suffering. You, who are qualifying for initiation, know why men are suffering, and may take the light of the spirit to souls in hell, to comfort them. This is work for everyone who has passed through initiation with understanding, whose eyes are opened. You can bear comfort to others. We speak most earnestly; today millions of souls are imprisoned in darkness; only those who have seen and gained understanding from the light can comfort these disquieted souls.

You will remember that the Master first spoke to a *woman* at the tomb, who represents the soul; this woman was the first to behold the Master, recognising that she had found something greater than herself. Even during the turmoil of the outer life the soul often feels that of itself it is empty, incomplete, longing for something wiser, more competent than itself to take over before it can be free. This something is the 'divine spark,' the pure Christ. The initiate, however, is aware at all times that he must allow this pure, this divine spark, to guide and command him.

Many of you say, 'How shall I know when the voice of pure truth is speaking to me and when it is only my lower self? How shall I know whether it is my guide or the imagining of my own mind?' We answer that both mind and soul have to learn to stand aside, to become very still in order to hear the voice of pure spirit—the Voice of the Silence, the soundless voice which needs no words, which speaks only truth, and through which you at once *know*. This is the voice of conscience and you cannot evade it, but must encourage and strive to develop it. In this way does the Master in us all rise from the dead.

After the resurrection something important follows. The Master said, 'Touch me not; for I am not yet ascended to my Father,' meaning that at that moment he could not bear contact with anything worldly because he was not then complete, had not become strong enough, and at that stage could be harmed by worldly men and worldly things. Some of you will understand this feeling. You have perhaps reached and beheld the heavenly glory for a moment, and yet you are not strong enough to stand up against corruption. The material touch, you feel intuitively, might damage you.

The final test, the final experience of ascension into the heavens, is the withdrawal of the higher from the denser self, and the transmutation of the bodily atoms so that the newly etherealised body becomes established, permanent—not in an earthly but a heavenly sense.

This is called the state of ascension, to which all Masters attain after the highest earthly initiation. The ascended Master having passed this high Earth Initiation whilst functioning in a physical body, so transmutes its fabric into light that to the man of earth the body seems to disappear in light.

Jesus arose from the dead! The very atoms of his physical body were changed and spiritualised. His body became transmuted from pain and darkness to light and freedom. Afterwards he walked and talked with his disciples and demonstrated to the world this triumph of spirit over matter. Then, having finished his mission, he was enveloped in light and was caught up into the heavens. In other words, he withdrew into that new life which, as we have described, will some day come both to individual man and to the earth itself.

We are able to speak of what we ourselves have seen concerning the future of mankind—of a life dawning for man which can only be described as celestial, when the light of the Son of God will shine through men's faces, when they will live without sickness, pain, want or suffering, a life harmonious and beautiful in every respect, warm and human, and where the fullest expression of the spirit can be given. Try to believe us if you can; try to believe that nothing is too good to be true. Believe in God, in good!

We say that wars shall cease; that untruth and ignorance will fade away; that human life will be lived from the centre of the Sun, from the heart of the Christ. There will be no more deception or illusion. The whole purpose of life here is the continued etherealisation of man and of the fabric of this earth. Do you know that there are already planets in existence in your solar system which have become so etherealised that they are outside the range of the most powerful telescopes? Yes, these are planets of light, bright and beautiful stars. This earth planet, very dark at present, is slowly quickening in vibration. This is where all you people have a great work waiting. So do not merely read our words and speedily forget them. Try to put into practice the Christ-thought; try to live the Christ life. Then you yourself will be aiding in the creation of a brighter world, and this dense matter, this darkness, will gradually be dissolved.

Do you now see why this universal drama of the crucifixion is continually being repeated, not only for followers of the Christian religion but for those of all other religions? For this is the drama of each man's soul-life, of his spiritual initiation from the darkness of physical matter to freedom and glory.

Great White Light, Eternal Spirit, Thou in

whom we live and move and have our being: we pray that the mists of confusion and illusion may be lifted so that we may behold the vision glorious, the vision of truth. May we, Thy children, come into the presence of Thy Son and take upon ourselves the soul of Christ, to live as He lives; and in His life may we become aware of the eternal presence of God. Amen.

THE WHITE EAGLE PUBLISHING TRUST

NEW LANDS · LISS · HAMPSHIRE